Samuel's Song

A Story of Rescue and Redemption

Beth Baird Smith

For Samuel

Jesus is King
Heaven is Home
And you're there waiting for us

Contents

From the Author	ix
1. A Face in the Forest	1
2. Smelling Safety	9
3. This is Home	15
4. Heading West	23
5. Being One of a Kind	35
6. To Remember Rainbows	45
7. Porches, Peas and Cornbread	57
8. Where the Trail Leads	69
9. Beyond the Woods	79
10. Mile Marker 183	89
11. Through a Window in Heaven	101
12. A Promise Kept	109
Afterword	115
Photo Gallery	119
Acknowledgments	125
About the Author	127

From the Author

TOPAZ eyes outlined in black study me from across the room. They don't seem to ask questions anymore, like they did in the autumn of 2017, and I feel a deep sense of gratitude as I watch her doze off peacefully.

She has been a gift, a lifeline, a tether to my sanity. She is the last and only link to what is gone from me, forever changing the landscape of my reality, and she seems to know it instinctively. Does she remember? What images might there be, permanently etched in her memory, of her life before? And what of that hot July day and the weeks that followed, before she came to snooze in the corner of my sofa? Is she even capable of such?

And I realize that, like so many other rhetorical questions and blanks that will never be filled in, I will probably never know. I don't really need to, and probably don't want to anyway. She is here now, and I am thankful for that and for the way she came to us.

God, the great rescuer of souls, created us in His image. That's why we all love a good rescue story - because HE does! He also loves to redeem the seemingly impossible. It's my hope and prayer that this story will compel you to run into the arms of your Rescuer and allow Him to redeem whatever you may think is hopeless. It is most definitely not.

Chapter 1

A Face in the Forest

The pungent smell of smoke roused her from sleep, reminding her of how hungry she'd become. She could make out her surroundings again, now that dawn was approaching, and she remembered why she was there, curled up under the thick brush where she had hidden herself the night before. She lifted her head slowly without making a sound and hoped whatever had been stalking her hours before had given up and gone away. It had. She was alone, just as she had been the day before... and the day before that? How long? She couldn't remember exactly when she had watched, from a hundred or more yards away, the farmer's old pickup truck hurriedly pulling away from the campsite in a cloud of dust, leaving her behind. Somehow the rabbit chase had taken her much farther away from the truck than she had thought, obviously beyond the sound of a call or whistle to her to return, and by the time she reached a clearing near the top of the hill to see the truck it was too late. She knew it wouldn't slow down for another look, and most likely would never return.

It had always felt that way, at least since the winter before when she was born into a large litter of pups on a small farm nestled in a quaint valley in the Ozark mountains. A large family had once lived there, growing crops and raising chickens and pigs. Farm dogs were necessary to protect the chickens from coyotes who roamed the area, but after the farmer's children were all grown and gone and his wife became ill and died, he could no longer manage the farm alone. The chickens and pigs were sold, as well as the farm equipment. When her litter was born he had no need to keep them all. She had watched helplessly as they had all disappeared, one by one, until she was the only one left. Her mother had been there with her for awhile, and then she too was gone. She knew she had seen the last of her mother when the farmer approached her with a familiar blue tattered collar and snapped it around her neck. It was too heavy for her small frame and she didn't want to wear it, but it smelled like her mother and comforted her. The old farmer didn't seem to care about much anymore and she noticed that he came outside less and less. Days would go by before the food bowl in the barn would appear with kibble in it. So when she had opportunity to jump in the back of the old pickup, she took it - oftentimes it meant she could find scraps from behind the diner in town or around the dumpsters before the truck would start up again, giving her just enough time to hop back in for the ride home. It wasn't much of a home, but it was all she knew.

On this particular day when the truck started down the driveway, it didn't head toward town. Instead, she rode under the rotting pile of hay and leaves for what seemed hours until it stopped in front of a fire pit in a little clearing encircled by woods. When the farmer spotted her jumping out of the truck that day, he scowled and shrugged his shoulders. She knew she'd have to keep a close watch on the truck this time if she wanted to get back to the barn, and she did - until she eyed the rabbit.

That was days, maybe weeks ago, and each time she returned to the campsite area hoping to find scraps of food left behind she was chased away by those of her kind who had been there much longer -

maybe all their lives - fighting for each meal, never knowing when the next one would come. They weren't about to share with her. Only the fittest survived here, and she instinctively knew she wouldn't last much longer. The barn and the empty bowl would've been a much better alternative. At least she was safe there, and eventually would get something to eat. The other farm animals knew her and seemed to pity her. But here, a hundred miles from familiarity, she had little chance.

As the light made it easier for her to see, she let her nose lead her closer to the smoke smell. Strange, she thought, that it would take her deeper and deeper into the woods and away from the campground area where normally one would find a fire. But there was no doubt she was headed the right way, and as she crept closer she saw the figure of a young man - on the thin side, and definitely younger than the farmer who had left her behind - poking at the fire with a long stick. He didn't seem to be in a hurry like most people always appeared to be, and he whistled a cheerful tune as he rearranged the last of the fire's embers, sometimes chuckling to himself out loud. The sight of him was inviting to her and she felt her fear subside. Did she dare? She knew it was a risk. But her belly ached, and she knew instinctively that where a man was, food couldn't be far away. She closed her eyes, thought again of her mother, and gingerly stepped forward out of the brush.

Samuel was a bit surprised to see her cautiously wander up to his campsite. After all, it was the middle of the week in late August and as far as he could tell, he was the only camper left there. Summer vacation was over, schools were back in session, and the colors of autumn were still a month away. Solitude.

He liked it that way, having the trails through the woods all to himself. The crunch of leaves on the forest floor, the snap of a twig as he brushed past an overhanging branch, and the occasional hissing of locusts in the trees reminded him of those late summer afternoons walking back to the creek behind his childhood home in central Louisiana. That was a simpler time, when his three older sisters tagged along beside him and his dad led the way, swatting away the horseflies and keeping a watch out for copperheads who liked to sunbathe just off the footpath.

His dad had lived within a few miles of there

since he too was a young boy, and had taken the opportunity to buy the 110 acres surrounded by national forest land when it presented itself. Soon thereafter, a new home place sprung up among the loblolly pines atop the hill. His parents had built it and moved into it together with three of his four siblings - a brother, 15 years his senior, and two younger sisters. Another sister followed within a couple of years, and then he - the youngest. The baby, the last one. He thought about how many times he wished he hadn't been the last, the one always having to hear what he wasn't allowed to do while the others could. *"You can't. You're not old enough yet."* Oh how he loathed it.

But the woods served as the great equalizer. In the safety of his dad's acreage he could run as fast as his five year old legs would carry him, ahead of his sisters and his dad and all the way back to their own private swimming hole on Big Creek. The water felt cool to his toes no matter how late in the summer it got, and he had his dad's permission to get in up to his knees before the others arrived. He'd make sure he was in as deep as he could go, and then he'd wait. He had loved that feeling, of being first in the creek. Being first meant there were less people around to tell you what to do.

But today he was well beyond those woods and Big Creek. The girls were grown and gone now, along with his older brother. His folks lived in another state, and the home place belonged to another family. Samuel was finding his own way in his own forest.

Chapter 2

Smelling Safety

The closer she got, the thinner he could see she was. "Alone for awhile out here," he muttered to himself, but audible enough for her to hear it. He figured she couldn't have been more than six months old, and he wondered who would decide, in a campground, to abandon a puppy without even removing her collar first. Surely she'd been lost - and her owner had looked and looked, unsuccessfully. But who wouldn't return, again and again, in the hopes of finding her? They could've at least put up a notice - most campgrounds had websites or facebook pages where guests could upload photos, comments or reviews of the park. He'd have to be sure to look online when he got within range of a cell signal. Letting her sniff his outstretched fingers on one hand, he used the other hand to reach out for the small tag attached to the collar around her neck. "JINX", it read. No address, no phone number. Just a name. *How fitting*, he thought. She reluctantly accepted the leftover bite of stale sandwich he offered her, then stayed alongside him as he broke camp and loaded his gear into the bed of the truck. When he opened the passenger door she jumped right up into the seat like she'd received an invitation. *Surely I'll see someone looking for her and calling for her*, he figured as he drove slowly throughout the campground. *Even though it sure looks like she's been out here awhile.* But there wasn't a vehicle to be seen. No one. It was just him and her, and he knew he couldn't leave her behind.

Reluctantly the boy pulled out onto the farm-to-market road heading away from the campground. He glanced at the passing utility poles, thinking he might see a homemade poster with "lost dog" across the top. Nothing. Mile after mile, the road remained as lonely as it had when he'd come to the campground days before. "Obviously no one's looking for a dog", he told his travel companion as he took a right turn onto the state highway. He considered the irony of the moment - thinking to himself about how anyone could just give up searching, if they had even searched at all, for a family pet. She did, after all, have a collar with a name on it. Someone had invested at least something in this puppy - unless they'd just had second thoughts and didn't want the responsibility anymore. All of the countless times his own family had called, texted, and tracked his phone - mostly his mom and sisters, sometimes his dad and older brother, looking for him and worrying about his whereabouts - began to make sense to him. Yet then, it had annoyed him to be the object of their searches. It never dawned on him that the reason might be because they cared. No, he was sure - he knew that was the reason. They'd all invested years of care, laughter and a lot of patience with him and he had no doubt of their love for him. An unexpected appreciation settled over him for the first time in awhile. He hummed under his breath, then began to sing an old Hank Williams classic that had been tucked away somewhere in the back of his memory. *"Why don't ya love me like ya use to do... why do ya treat me like a worn out shoe?"* His new friend sighed, rested her head on the seat beside him and drifted off to sleep at the sound of his gentle voice. Finishing his tune and wistfully remembering how he and his dad had crooned it together on countless car rides and walks in the woods, he looked down at her and spoke reassuringly, "You'll never be farther than a country mile from me, little girl. You're mine now." He already loved the feeling of being needed, depended on, appreciated. He knew she felt safe with him, after heaven only knew what kind of trauma she'd endured alone out in those woods. He wondered if his mother had the same sense of fulfillment when she knew her children needed her and they welcomed her love. He would make a concentrated effort to call her when he got home. It had been awhile. Too long.

Hunger still gnawed at her empty belly each time she was roused awake by the truck tires hitting a pothole, but the relief she felt just by being with the boy surpassed her desire to eat. It had been weeks, it seemed, since she had felt safe in the farmer's barn where she'd been raised with her mother and her siblings. And although she'd been the only one left, familiarity was still a welcomed friend to her. But after days and days of returning to the site where she had jumped out of the back of the farmer's truck only to find it not there, she intuitively knew her life at the barn was over and she'd never be back there. The steady hum of the wheels on the asphalt lulled her into as deep of a sleep as she'd been in for a long time, and she dreamed of her mother loping alongside her in the pasture until she had no energy left to run. Collapsing into the tall meadow grass, her mother would drop down beside her and they'd doze together under an endless blue sky until grasshoppers would tickle them both awake.

But today, miles from what she knew as home, a strange hand caressed her ears and stroked her back as she lay next to him on the dusty front seat of the truck. She inched closer, pressing her nose into his dirt-crusted blue jeans so she could remember the smell of him. It wouldn't have been pleasant to another human, more than likely. She could tell he'd gone without a bath for a few days. But to her it was comforting. Beyond the smell, though, there was something else. Because the human body emits a certain scent, undetectable to people but unmistakable to animals, they're alerted to emotions - both negative and positive - and will interpret them as either a warning or a clearance. She was picking up the distinct redolence of warmth and acceptance from him. Instinctively, she knew what it was - even though she'd never detected it coming from a human in her world. His long slender fingers felt reassuring and comforting to her, and she leaned into them. Home would now be wherever the boy was, and she hadn't a clue where that would be. It didn't much matter to her anyway. She drifted off again, knowing already she was loved.

Chapter 3
This is Home

It was another hour on the road toward Little Rock before he would have a strong enough signal to call the house. He knew he'd have to ask his brother about bringing a stray dog home before he just showed up. Ray had his own dog, a sweet gentle Doberman he had named Caillou, and the house rules had been made clear to Samuel several months before. "I'm not having Cai fixed, so this is a one-dog home," he'd declared emphatically. So he would have to play his cards right if he had any chance of keeping his new friend and continuing to be roommates with his older brother. Fortunately for Samuel, Ray was as much or more of a dog-lover than he - so he figured the odds were in his favor. He scrolled down on his flip phone and hit the call button. The deep familiar voice picked up on the other end with the usual, "Hey Dewey! What's up and where are you?"

"Dewey" had been the name Ray most liked calling him, and Samuel loved the uniqueness of it. No other family member had earned a nickname from his brother and it made him feel special. It wasn't actually a nickname, but rather a form of his given middle name, Deward, which was his maternal grandfather's name and the name of two generations before his grandfather. His mother was one of two sisters - no brothers to continue the name - so, being the last boy born in his grandfather's line, he inherited the unusual name. Ray, not realizing that their great-great grandfather had actually gone by the name "Dewey", playfully coined numerous variations of Deward and had landed on this one. It stuck, and further endeared his little brother - 15 years his junior - to him.

Ray's greeting brought a smile to Samuel as he prepared a sales speech in his mind. "Hey man," he began. "Got a huge favor to ask." He heard a faint sigh on the other end of the phone. Favors had been handed out to him on a regular basis lately - especially from his older brother, who had reluctantly agreed to let Samuel move to Little Rock with him because staying home with his parents wasn't exactly working out. Ray was too much older to just be a buddy, and had sown enough of his own wild oats at Samuel's age that he had long since settled into the role of an adult with a full-time job and a mortgage to pay. Living with Ray gave him just the right balance of accountability and freedom to be independently on his own. They'd agreed to split the utility bills down the middle, and Samuel would be responsible for his own groceries. He assumed some of the household jobs and adhered to the general rules that Ray had made. Samuel knew he was serious, and that getting too close to the line could mean eviction - even from his brother. Ray loved him - enough to take him in, give him lots of grace, be a sounding board since he'd been through much of the same struggles - but he wouldn't put up with foolishness.

The silence grew long on the other end, so he continued. "So, this pup found me at the campground, and no one was around, and I checked, and it was hungry, and you know YOU wouldn't have been able to leave it there, so I...well, you know. And it's just TEMPORARY, till I can find a home for it. Unless you decide you like her. I mean IT." Oops, he knew he'd messed up with that mistake. Ray zeroed in on the error. "SHE?? You did just say SHE, didn't you?" "Well yes, but I'll keep her in the backyard, and anyways she's only a few months old so Cai probably won't even be interested..." He waited through another several seconds of silence. "Okay Dew, but ONLY until you find another home for her. And I mean it!" The line went dead, and 30 minutes later Samuel pulled into Ray's driveway knowing he'd have a lot more convincing to do if there were any possibility under heaven of him keeping this sweet girl who had not lifted her head off of his lap for the past two hours. He'd think of something. He always did.

She knew immediately, as most dogs do, that she had no need to fear Cai, this gentle giant of a dog - though he towered above her on all fours. He could've crushed her but he didn't seem to know it or even care. It felt good to be around another one of her kind who didn't feel threatened with the need to protect his turf or food source, and this guy was a big teddy bear who loved head scratches and snuggles on the sofa with any human who would oblige him. She watched the interaction between Cai and Samuel, then the warm, strong bond between the boy with his brother, and she realized how much better of a situation for her this was than to be back at the farm with an old man who thought so little of her. Thank goodness he hadn't cared enough to come back to look around the campground. That part of her life was over. She figured anything else had to be an improvement. Maybe the older brother would warm to her the way the younger one had, and she could stay. She hoped.

The changing season brought cooler mornings and evenings, and the two brothers found more time to go on long walks through the woods adjacent to the neighborhood. Cai had obviously been well-trained to come back to Ray immediately when called, so they'd let both dogs off their leashes when they knew there'd be no one else around. She'd stay close to Cai as he ran and jumped through the high grasses, but his legs were much longer and stronger so it was an effort to keep up. The last thing she wanted was to get lost, to be left behind, so she resisted the temptation to follow a scent that would lead her away from Cai. When she heard the familiar whistle, she wasted no time getting back to the boys. Cai always managed to get there ahead of her no matter how fast she ran, but they always watched and waited for her. She loved knowing they'd never turn and leave her, forgetting about her. She was becoming part of their pack.

A month or two passed, and the Arkansas nights turned cooler. Ray seemed to relax about having a second dog around, but she still feared her days there were numbered - the wooden porch rails Ray had just stained had her fresh chew marks on most of them, her puppy-way of protesting the long days when the brothers both went to work and Cai was content to snooze the day away on the couch indoors. She'd been fine, at first, to sleep out on the backyard deck since coming to live here, but now Samuel took her to the garage at night where it was warmer and she could sleep on an old blanket. She didn't mind - it was all she knew, being born in a barn and never going inside a house where people lived. The fenced-in yard made her feel safe during the daytime, and she knew every afternoon that Samuel would appear at the door with a bowl of food, his cheerful voice would greet her, and most times when the temperature was pleasant enough, he'd play in the yard with her until it got too dark to see. The days would be long, waiting for him to come home, but the sun-drenched deck was the perfect spot to nap when she wasn't digging along the fence line or chasing squirrels into the trees. She loved her life here, and thoughts of the farmer, the old barn, and her mother dimmed in her memory.

Now that it appeared she'd be staying, Samuel needed a name for her. "Jinx" definitely wouldn't work. He'd tossed that name tag before he got back to Ray's house, not wanting to be reminded of how unlucky she'd have undoubtedly become if she'd stayed in the woods alone. Oddly enough and for some strange reason, the Hebrew language had intrigued him for the past couple of years - after all, that's where his own first name had originated - so he'd google-searched websites to study the origin of names, looking for something that would be easy enough to say but would have significant meaning to him, too. She probably would've died, eventually, living out in the wild where the campground was, not able to fight off predators. He came across a word that meant "life, living"- CHAVA - and thought about the life he'd probably saved when he brought her home. He said the Hebrew name over and over to himself, then looked at her. "CHAVA," he commanded. Immediately she jumped to her feet and was at his side. "That's what it is, then," Samuel told her. "And just to be sure it's pronounced the way it's supposed to be, I'll replace the C with a K. Your name is Khava."

It would be the next autumn before someone would discover another Hebrew word pronounced the same way - with a meaning that Samuel had apparently missed. Or had he?

Chapter 4

Heading West

November came and went, and so did Samuel's job with the landscaping crew at the golf course. "Seasonal," he'd been told, although he had hoped there'd be something he could do for the company beyond merely mowing the greens. Money was getting tight, and the agreement with Ray about sharing and covering expenses still stood and hung over him. He figured he had just enough saved to take him through December until the beginning of January.

Confirmation came for Samuel that it was time to move on when Ray decided to put his house on the market and move to Florida. He'd started dating someone there, and this girl was worth the trouble of relocating, finding another job, and starting over. He sensed this relationship would be permanent. Samuel could sense it too, and couldn't help but be happy for his 34 year old brother whom he knew was ready to settle down. Robin had been a family friend for over a decade, had taught and coached their sisters in high school, and already had the votes of everyone in the family to come aboard. Ray had been spending more and more time on the phone at night with her and Samuel knew his brother's heart had been won over.

The house sold quickly, and as Samuel helped with the packing process he began to consider his own plans. He hadn't thought much about it, but the itch to be on the road and explore a myriad of possibilities beckoned him, even in the middle of a cold, bleak Arkansas winter. He could go home, to Florida, stay with Ray for awhile once he got settled in somewhere, or live with his parents if he could find a job. He knew they'd gladly welcome Khava - but he also realized that wouldn't last very long. He could go a few hours east, to Nashville where his oldest sister lived and always made him feel loved and welcomed. Rachel listened to him ramble on with his conspiracy theories about chemtrails in the skies and how the government kept spying on everyone, but she also loved to sit and just hear him dream. The nine year gap in their ages gave her more patience and understanding for him, and he didn't feel so much like the annoying little brother anymore. He thought about it briefly, but no - it was time to head in a different direction. He wanted to venture west, where he'd never gone before, and this time he had a traveling companion to keep him company - who needed him as much as he needed her. He spent one dreary, drizzly day in early January studying the US map and searching the internet for farms that needed volunteers to come do seasonal work in exchange for a place to stay and a meal or two a day. He knew he'd have to find a farm that would let him bring Khava, so most were ruled out - but he found a place in Utah that looked intriguing.

The following day he loaded up his truck, bid his goodbyes to Ray and Caillou, grabbed a half-loaf of bread and a jar of peanut butter, made room for Khava to sit in the seat beside him, and headed west on Interstate 40 toward the wide-open Great Plains with the Utah mountains ahead, waiting for him on the other side of a long, lonely stretch of nothingness. The adventure of unfamiliarity was calling again, and like always, he couldn't resist it.

* * *

Her legs cramped in the small front seat next to him, but his hand resting on her neck reassured her that all was well as the hours dragged by and the hum of the engine kept lulling her back to sleep. An unusually bright winter sun warmed her through the windshield - she hadn't remembered this much sunshine while back in Arkansas, where most days this time of year were gray and damp. When she heard the truck slow down and pull over every few hours, she knew it meant a gas stop and a break for her - time to stretch her legs and sniff around to see who had been here before her arrival. Only a few minutes though, and it was back in the front seat for more hours of chasing the sun as it led the way for them on the horizon, gradually sinking out of sight and making way for the darkness that would soon follow. She wasn't really sure how many nights they stopped in roadside parks where Samuel would pitch a small tent for them, roll out his sleeping bag and, after making a peanut butter sandwich for both of them, they'd drift off to sleep to the sound of chirping crickets and an occasional truck whose driver had decided to continue on through the night. It felt wonderful to stretch out on the cool ground beneath the tent and hear the boy's steady breathing as he slept.

    One afternoon, just before the sun slipped down

behind the terrain in front of them, he turned off the main highway onto a bumpy, gravel road - much like the road she remembered at the farm where she had lived as a puppy. "Mystic Hot Springs, two miles ahead," she heard him mutter under his breath as he squinted in the afternoon sun to see the rusty sign on the side of the road. "That's our landing place, sweet girl," he whispered to her softly. "At least for now."

Pulling through the gate felt like stepping back into a time period he'd only heard about from people his parents' age or older - those who'd grown up in the 60's and 70's, who remembered Woodstock and Jimi Hendrix and knew exactly where they were when JFK was assassinated. Campsites, rustic cabins and even converted old school buses dotted the rocky terrain around him. Occasionally he'd pass one or two old-timers walking along the gravel road - "gray-haired hippies", he explained to Khava as if he knew what she'd ask him if she could. This was definitely not a farm. It looked more like a haven, a refuge for those who'd been thrown into a future they didn't want to be living in, deplete of peace and love and tie-dyed t-shirts. Misfits, like him, who didn't belong in the current culture of high-speed technology and the need to succeed. But these were misfits from another previous generation who had found each other. Where were the misfits in society who had yet to turn 20? He knew of none.

The road ended at a small unassuming cabin with a long front porch cluttered with wooden rockers, rusted bicycles, terra cotta flowerpots and at least a dozen pairs of flip-flops in front of the door. A sign dangled from a strand of rusty wire above the door: "MIKE". He rolled the windows down and turned off the truck. "Wait here," he instructed Khava, and he walked up to the screen door and pushed it open.

"Mystic Mike" was anything but mystic. He looked more like an over-baked ranch hand that hadn't seen a razor in a few weeks, but his eyes twinkled curiously when he looked up to see a skinny teenaged boy with hair that flipped up at his shoulders wearing a dirt-smudged t-shirt and baggy jeans and an ear-to-ear grin. "I'm Sam Smith," the boy began as he stuck out his hand toward Mike. "We talked last week on the phone." Mike sat a minute before he answered. "Ahh, yes... you're the kid willing to shovel manure in exchange for room and board. Well, I've got the work for ya, but the room... I don't. If you've got a tent, you can pitch it over yonder. And we serve one meal a day in the back here. No promises on edibility." He chuckled, but the boy didn't. "That'll work for us," he said. "Us?" Mike asked. "Me and Khava, my dog. She's always part of the package." A leathery smile broke out on Mike's face. "Just keep her away from my chickens," he told him. "And meet me at the llama pen at 7am sharp. Plan to smell as bad as the llamas." Samuel figured he probably already did.

Walking back to where yonder apparently was located, he noticed again the old school buses randomly perched here and there. Curiosity got the better of him and he got close enough for a look inside a couple of them. On the walls, scribbled in Sharpie markers, he read quotes that instantly made him feel connected with whomever these oddities were around here.

"My heart swings back and forth between the need for routine and the urge to run."

"A mind stretched by new experiences can never go back to its old dimensions:

TRAVEL. LEARN. GROW."

And then a quote from a popular song by The Grateful Dead:

"Once in awhile you get shown the light, in the strangest of places if you look at it right."

Mornings in the Utah mountains were cooler than he had expected. At daybreak, the smell of coffee drew him out of his sleeping bag to pull on his jeans and flannel shirt and head out of the tent to where the source of the smell was coming from. He hoped someone would be kind enough to share, and they were. After a cup of what his Dad would've called "sock coffee" (because it tasted like it had dripped straight out of the aforementioned), Samuel and Khava headed toward the llama pens. They weren't hard to find - the stench pointed them in the right direction. Mike was already there waiting and handed the boy a shovel and showed him the wheelbarrow. At least a dozen llama stood perfectly still, watching, until the dog crept closer - and they trotted off, hoping not to be followed. "Plenty of poop to keep you busy for the morning," Mike laughed, and off he went. Khava chose to stay close to Samuel as he started shoveling - until she spotted the chickens coming to see what had stirred up the llamas, and her instincts got the best of her. By the time Samuel could put his shovel down, she'd caught one in her teeth and was headed under the fence with it, but he managed to grab her by the neck until she dropped it. "This ain't gonna work," he fussed. "Guess I'll have to get the rope and tie you up at the tent."

* * *

She hated the rope, because it meant the boy wouldn't be close by anymore and she had no idea when he'd return. She could faintly hear his whistling though, and it reassured her that he was near. Every once in awhile he'd break into a song, then it would stop when she heard the clang of the shovel against the side of the wheelbarrow. Soon enough he'd start up again, and she thought it strange that a human would enjoy being around animals and not be in a hurry to get away. She loved that he always seemed content and happy doing whatever he was doing. And he was always glad to see her when he finished, making it a priority to see that she had food to eat, water to drink and a place to rest. That's all he seemed to want, too. Simplicity and peace. How had she gotten so lucky?

The next morning he gave her another chance at resisting the urge to chase the chickens, but instinct again got the best of her and she ended up right back where she'd found herself the day before - tied up by the tent. A third chance the next day and it happened again, so there were no more chances given and she knew she'd have to wait at the tent until the shoveling was done, the pen was clean and her smelly, sweaty companion shuffled back to the tent for a nap. Afternoons took them both on long walks around the property and sometimes up into the red hills, where he'd let her off the leash to chase whatever critters were curious enough to let her see them. They'd wander back to the campsite in time for the boy to shower at the outdoor spigot and put on a clean t-shirt for dinner. An hour later, he'd be back with whatever scraps he could tuck into a paper napkin and sneak out of the building. It wasn't much, but it was enough. She'd never had it better, and didn't figure she could find a kinder soul than this one who had brought her home, changed her name, and called her his.

Another week or so went by, and one evening the boy returned to their campsite walking slower than usual, head lowered, without the usual cheery whistling she was accustomed to hearing. She wondered what had changed. "Time to move on, sweet girl," he told her as he patted her head and gave her his scraps. "Too many upset chickens and not enough llama poop. We hit the road in the morning." And sure enough, when day broke, he rolled up the tent and loaded his few belongings up in the truck, waved at a few folks sipping their morning coffee, and the two of them drove off in the red dust headed somewhere, but together. He was whistling again, so she didn't much care where that would be or how long it would take. When they turned onto the highway a few miles down the dirt road, Samuel reached for the flip phone he'd kept under the truck seat and pushed in some numbers. She heard a faint ringing. "Hey Dad," he spoke quietly. "Don't really wanna get into it, but I'm leaving Utah. Think I'll head to Texas."

Chapter 5

Being One of a Kind

Until recently he'd have dreaded making that phone call to his father. Dad always had a better plan, one that made more sense, at least to himself. But not to Samuel. He'd grown weary of listening to everyone else's plans and ideas for him about where he should live, go to school (or not, but that was only HIS plan), work a job - why was he expected to conform to their standards on what was best? His definition of "best" wasn't theirs. Sure, he'd made mistakes, errors in judgment, sometimes costing him significantly - but he was clear of all those now, and had his whole life in front of him. He knew what NOT to do, and what rules he'd have to follow to not burn bridges with people who loved him and wanted to help him. Those were small prices to pay for the freedom that he now had, as long as his pickup truck was running and his mom kept his cell phone on her plan. He didn't really worry about that part. Mom was in his corner, always giving him the benefit of the doubt, believing the best in him, hoping and praying he'd be safe and that someday, he'd find his passion and his purpose. She knew once he found it he'd pour himself into it and succeed. He realized, of course, he'd be limited by not having any college education - but there was no way on earth that would happen. Samuel's education was beyond his windshield, between the horizon and clouds, and he'd know it when he saw it. He had to look at things practically though, since gas didn't stay in his tank miraculously. Food didn't appear in the styrofoam ice chest in his back seat unless he bought it and put it there. Those essentials required money, and it helped to have connections when looking for ways to make some. He had family in Texas, grandparents and an aunt who adored him and two cousins who were actually a lot of fun and didn't seem to be bothered by his nonconformity. His mom and dad had just informed him they'd be selling the home in Florida and moving to Texas themselves, to be near his grandparents, and where his dad would take a job working with a friend. So Texas just seemed like a good direction in which to head.

He met no resistance when he asked for enough gas and food money to get him to his grandparents' home in Fort Worth. He was even slightly receptive to his dad's suggestion that he let him check out farms in the central Texas area that might be looking for help while he drove the long hours heading south, stopping only for short breaks to rest at roadside rest areas where he didn't have internet access to look on his own . *Okay*, he mused to himself. *I'll let Dad look and call and find just the right place - in his opinion - for me to work. And then I'll do what I want to do.*

It had been a long, grueling day in the front seat of the truck and Khava's legs ached. She felt restless and sensed there were more new people to meet, creating a bit of uncertainty in her about the permanency of her relationship with the boy. Would he grow tired of having her around, always with him, needing to be cared for? The farmer she had belonged to had made her distrusting of people. He'd taken away all the other pups from her litter and finally, even her mother until she was the only dog left on the property. He tolerated her at best. She kept rats out of his barn, alerted him to coyotes who ventured onto the farm and threatened the chickens, and didn't bother him when he'd forgotten to put food in her bowl. She always managed to find a broken egg or two on the ground, or some extra slop the pigs didn't quite finish. She'd done her best to be worthy of staying on the farm, but still... that farmer couldn't have cared less when she wasn't in the bed of his truck at the time he left the campground. Dogs were easy to come by. He'd find a replacement soon enough.

But Samuel wasn't like the farmer, or any other people she'd been around. He had talked to her for hours as they'd made their way down lonely highways headed to wherever he'd decided they were going. His voice was tender and soothing, and she knew he enjoyed her company. She could hear the inflection in his voice change and instinctively knew he was asking her a question, but all she could do was lick his hand and stare into his piercing eyes that seemed to be expecting her to answer. She never dared look the farmer directly in the eyes, but Samuel seemed to love holding her gaze and many times, they'd just stare at one another without him ever saying a word. She learned to read him, to know his moods by the length of his stares at her. So when he pulled into the driveway of his grandparents' home, she dreaded the emotional separation she knew she'd feel when she had to share her beloved companion with others who vied for his attention. He whistled at her as he stepped out of the truck. Puzzled to be invited, she jumped out and followed him to the front door of the home his grandparents had lived in for as long as he could remember.

Ringing the doorbell, a warmth spread over Samuel as he reflected back over his nineteen years of being the youngest of their seven grandchildren, and always feeling a bit special because of it. For the majority of those years, he'd lived hundreds of miles away in Florida and was only there to visit a couple of times a year at best. But his grandparents loved to travel, particularly to Florida and especially during cold Texas winters and the equally as brutal scorching summers. He loved it when they'd come and stay, because it always brought a change in routine and life seemed to slow down when they visited. His grandfather, whom Ray had named

"Dadad" when he wasn't quite old enough to pronounce "Grand-dad", enjoyed taking Samuel to do things with him that his older sisters had no interest in doing. He remembered one summer day the two of them venturing off to an outdoor air museum to spend an afternoon looking at old fighter planes used during World War II. Dadad had been a young boy when the U.S. entered the war, and had joined the Marine Corps shortly after his high school graduation. He'd tried college briefly, but struggled to make the grades and lacked focus. When the Vietnam war started, he and a buddy had the bright idea of joining the Marines in order to avoid possibly being drafted into the Army - which, they assumed, would be much harder than serving as a Marine. They enlisted one day, told their families the next, and headed west on a bus for Camp Pendleton on the California coast. It was there that Dadad met his lifelong love and future wife, a 19 year old Kentucky girl spending the summer after her freshman year at Union College out on the Oceanside beach with her older sister, a schoolteacher. They married less than a year later and returned together to Texas, where Dadad would enroll again as a college student - and this time, prove to be successful at it. Samuel's mom was born that next year, and Dadad would go to work full-time for the family business. Although he never flew, he still loved old vintage planes and was delighted when his youngest grandson showed an interest himself. Maybe some of it was just a natural curiosity the boy had for his namesake.

Samuel had always considered it an honor to carry the name Deward, knowing that the three men in his lineage who shared it with him had helped to lead and guide a successful family business that earned a stellar reputation in the state of Texas. He loved hearing the story of his great-great-great grandmother who founded that business, and how her entrepreneurial spirit helped her provide for not just her own children but for many descendants to come. She was one of a kind in her time, and he liked that about her. Being one of a kind meant you were different, not cut out of the same cloth as most folks.

Both she and her husband had been orphaned, not a particularly unusual thing back in the 1800's, and had married young. By the time she was 26 years old, she had buried two of her four children. They soon decided it was time to move south to Texas from their home in Tennessee, where her husband William purchased a steam-engined popcorn machine on a cart and began his business in the dirt streets of downtown Fort Worth. But tragedy struck the young family again when William died at the age of 44, leaving his wife Ninnie a widow with eight young children to feed and raise. Undaunted by adversity, she turned her love for baking homemade bread into a thriving business that would provide a livelihood for generations to come and bring steady jobs to countless Texans in major cities throughout the state. Mrs. Baird's Bakeries would grow to become the largest and most successful family-owned bread business in the nation. One little lady left her mark on a slice of history, and five generations later, Samuel Deward Smith wondered if he could leave even half as significant a mark on his world as she had left on hers.

Standing on his grandparents front porch, he smiled, reflecting back on his day at the air museum and recalling the tour guide asking questions to the group about which plane was which and what each was used for, and how he knew the answers when no one else did. Dadad loved bragging on his then 10 year old grandson "who knew more about those planes than anyone else in the crowd, including the tour guide". He loved knowing his grandfather was proud of him, and smiled again at the thought of Ray always calling him Dewey. And even through some turbulent years as a young teen, he knew that both of his grandparents loved him and believed the best about him. Nothing inside of him made him wonder whether or not he'd be welcomed at this house today, and when the door opened, he was certain of it.

Chapter 6

To Remember Rainbows

The familiar scent surprised her yet again as she trotted in behind him, sticking closely beside him and being careful so she wouldn't be shown the door to the backyard. Separation, however temporary, had to be avoided and was a risk she simply could not take. She couldn't lose him. But that scent - the same one she encountered when Samuel brought her into Ray's house - was unmistakeable. She sensed the connectedness and her instincts told her these people were all part of the same pack. They were good, and they could be trusted. She could relax. Stretching out on the soft carpeting, she rested her head across the top of the boy's boots and dozed off peacefully while he chatted and laughed for what must have been hours.

Later there would be food - even for her - and the day ended with her being allowed to sleep at the foot of his bed, safe and secure and hoping this would never come to an end. For a split second, just before she drifted off to sleep for the night, she thought she could feel the slight brush of her mother's wet nose against her face - as if to reassure her that all was well.

Samuel heard his cell phone ring early the next morning and he knew it could only be one person - his dad, mainly because he knew of no one else awake before dawn. He also knew his father loved to "help" - sometimes too much - and that Samuel didn't give him much opportunity anymore to do so. He'd asked him, just the day before, for extra funds and had reluctantly agreed to let him look online for working farms that may need a hand - and that would allow a dog. So when the call came, Samuel figured his dad had some prospects. Sure enough, Dad had located a small farm a few miles outside of Cameron and just west of the Brazos River where a farmer needed help rebuilding four large greenhouses that had been shredded by a recent tornado.

He needed to set up an aquaponics system in at least two of them and was pressed for time because it was already growing season. A bunkhouse was empty and available on the back of the 150 acres, with a bed, bathroom, small living area and kitchen. He could live and eat free of charge as payment for work for the first month, then they'd talk. Samuel agreed to drive down and meet the owner, so later that morning he loaded Khava and his things in the truck and they took off for Cameron. The drive south was more beautiful than he'd expected it to be - lush and green, rolling hills and lots of wide open space. This was typical Texas countryside. He could breathe, see the horizon both east and west, and the expansive freedom was invigorating to his senses. He had a good feeling about this, and hoped the farmer would have the same.

No one just "happened" by this farm. One had to know exactly where he was going and be highly intentional about getting there. He followed the map on his phone until he lost service, then had to back track a mile or so until he could pull up the map again and take a snapshot of his destination. *Good thing I don't talk or text much*, he thought to himself, *because it sure won't be happening on this farm*. He'd have to drive the two or three miles back to the farm-to-market highway to get reception again. But he didn't mind much. He liked the feeling of being untethered. The interview with the farmer went well, although Samuel wasn't anticipating the list of rules that the farmer was insistent upon being followed - one of which was "absolutely no smoking on the farm". *Well,* he reasoned, *I suppose now is as good of a time as any to quit.* He'd already stopped eating meat the year before after working for three weeks on a cattle ranch and seeing first hand some things he wished he hadn't. *Not for me*, he had determined. So the cigarettes would be the next unhealthy habit to go. And there were others: no cursing, be on time, keep the bunkhouse clean. He figured he could manage those, and for the most part, he did.

Work started right away, the following morning. He loved working until his shoulders ached and his white pocket t-shirt was drenched in sweat. It made him feel productive and gave him a strong sense of fulfillment. He thought about his friends back in Florida, where he'd gone to school until he just couldn't sit in a classroom anymore and found a way to get out - for good - no matter how much his parents had tried to make him continue. He thought about them all, squirming at their desks and staring out windows at the world outside, where he was and they weren't. All for what? A piece of paper, after four years, telling you and whoever else cared that you knew how to do something so you could get a paycheck and then exchange that hard-earned money for things that cost too much money? No way. He wasn't about to waste his life away doing what everyone else did. He may have dirt under his fingernails and smell - as his middle sister liked to say - like a monkey cage, but he was happy and doing what he loved. He was learning what he needed until he knew what to do and then could move on to the next lesson, in the next place, on the next adventure. Would there be enough life to see and do and experience everything he wanted to do? Something in him burned to keep searching, to keep going, to keep looking. There was more. His soul unmistakably knew it.

In the meantime, there were practical matters that had to be tended to. Sweaty clothes needed washing and dog food had to be replenished. Saturday mornings took the two of them east, crossing the Brazos River and heading into Calvert to a laundromat. On one of their Saturday drives, Samuel watched something fly out of the window of a car in front of him and into the roadside ditch. He couldn't believe he'd seen what he did. *A kitten? Someone would purposely throw a kitten out of a moving vehicle?* He slowed to a stop and ran back towards the place he figured the kitten had landed. And there it was - stunned, but still breathing. He scooped it up and held it close, up to his chest. It appeared to be unhurt, miraculously. *Well, little buddy, you get a second chance. You get ME.* It was an easy introduction between the kitten and Khava, as she seemed to instinctively know someone new had joined their pack. "Say hello to Chance," he told her. "After all, everybody deserves one."

Days turned into weeks before he knew it. Spring seemed to end one day and the heat announcing another Texas summer appeared the next. One greenhouse was now full with a complete aquaponics system and a second one was almost ready. Life was everywhere - green and lush, growing and changing before his eyes. A sense of pride made his heart swell as he surveyed what he'd been able to accomplish in such a short amount of time. *Yes*, he nodded and told himself. *This is the life I was made for. The life I want, and the life I'll have.*

He'd even given his parents, in Texas for the Easter weekend, a tutorial tour of his working greenhouse and had spent the better part of a day just enjoying their company. He knew they were relieved to see him this content, this peaceful. It had been a long time coming. "I'll do my best to make it up to Ft. Worth for Easter Sunday services," he had told them as they got in the car to leave. He meant it this time, and he made it happen. It was the first church service he'd attended in a long time, and it felt familiar and safe. It felt like home. He missed that feeling.

For the first several days, Khava couldn't have been happier. Room to run, the boy within eyesight at all times, getting to sleep inside the bunkhouse with him - a dog's heaven. But the puppy in her got the best of her and she couldn't keep herself away from "new friends" in the nearby barn that didn't exactly share her sentiments. The farmer and his young family also had a dog and she suddenly became the "bad influence", a nuisance to the children and consequently a distraction to Samuel who was busy with greenhouse repairs and had to continually stop to deal with her. So she found herself tied up on a long rope to a tree just outside of the bunkhouse and half a mile away from where he was working all day. The rope - and the separation - were grim reminders to her of a year earlier and she tried desperately to get free, to get to the boy who had saved her life and who now was her life. Feverishly she chewed through each rope he would replace until he had to resort to a cable that she couldn't conquer. She knew he hated doing it, but she also could see that he was happy - learning more about what he loved to do and coming back to the bunkhouse sweaty, exhausted, but content. She knew it was a sacrifice worth making, because he was worth it. She would wait, and he would return. Usually, Chance the kitten waited with her. Every late afternoon she'd hear the familiar whistling as he came over the hill, back to her. She wasn't sure how much time had passed since she had stopped chewing through ropes and had settled into lazy days sleeping under the shade of a sprawling oak, content to lie in the thick grass, listening for the sound of his whistle... weeks, maybe? But one afternoon she heard his footsteps and no whistling. His footfall seemed softer, slower, and he was silent. She sensed the difference and knew something had shifted. Was it her? Would she lose him? He trudged up the steps to the bunkhouse and went inside, closing the door behind him. She wanted desperately to chew, to sever the cable that kept her from him, no matter how much pain it would cause her to do it. He was everything to her and she couldn't think about not being with him. So when he finally emerged from the bunkhouse and walked over to let her off of the cable, she heard him almost whisper to her: "Time to go again, girl. We gotta leave Chance behind, but you and me are a team. You'll always go where I go."

The conversation with the farmer had been short and abrupt and he wasn't budging. "You broke one too many of my rules," he kept saying, "and I can't let you stay any longer. Time to move on." Samuel knew he was in deep water a few days earlier when he let one of his homegrown expletives slip in front of the farmer's young daughter, quietly standing behind him when the hammer in his hand hit his thumb instead of the intended nail. But they had talked, he and the farmer, and he assumed all was forgiven. Apparently though, not all was forgotten. "Pack up your things from the bunkhouse and I'll expect you to be gone by lunchtime," the boy heard him say. It had been awhile since he'd fought back tears but now they fell freely and uncontrollably. He had a sudden, strong desire to call his dad, so he did. He could barely explain what had happened when his dad answered the phone, and his tears turned to sobs. "Can you please call him, Dad? Can you just try?" Samuel knew if anyone could talk someone off of a ledge, it was his father - fifteen years a lawyer and a term in the state legislature had afforded him the gift of gab, and the boy had picked up a good bit of it growing up under his dad, forty years his senior. But he had tried his hand at convincing the farmer to no avail. Now it was Dad's turn. "Sit tight, Samuel. I'll get back to you in a few minutes."

When his dad called back, it wasn't with the news he had hoped he'd get. The farmer was undaunted, even by an older man's pleas to give his son one more chance. Broken hearted, the boy headed back down to the bunkhouse to pack up the few things he had brought with him and his beloved dog. He would drive back to his grandparents' home in Ft. Worth and figure it out. His cell phone rang once he got onto the main highway. It was his mother, worried about him and wanting to be sure he was okay to make the drive. "I'm okay now Mom. Got my chin up and my sights on the next place I'm suppose to be."

* * *

This time Khava knew she was welcome here, and she was grateful for the warm, soft wall-to-wall carpet and the cool air conditioning. When the front door opened she trotted in ahead of him. "Hello again Miss Khava," she heard a warm soft voice say from behind her. She glanced back to see Samuel in his grandfather's arms, not even having stepped over the threshold yet. The entire afternoon must have drifted by as she slept, and though she hadn't a clue what the next thing would be, she was sure it would be all right. For the next two weeks, Samuel would leave the house each morning and return some eight hours later, sweaty and smelly. He'd been working somewhere, she knew. His aunt had lined him up with some light construction work and he was happy to have it while he waited on his next venture. After a shower and the evening meal, he would treat her to a long walk across the Benbrook Lake Dam to watch the most brilliantly-colored sunsets she'd ever noticed. Sometimes after a late afternoon thunderstorm, a rainbow would appear in the clouds above the lake, mixing with the hues of the sunset when the clouds would part enough to reveal the masterpiece behind them. "That's God showing off again,"

Samuel would tell her, just like he'd told his dad as a boy when they'd watch Florida sunsets and rainbows over Lake Jessup. She loved them because he did, and he would tell her about every color and why rainbows were symbolic and why it was important to have promises we could count on. He didn't think much about her understanding what he told her, but she did. And she would remember.

Chapter 7

Porches, Peas and Cornbread

Dad was making calls again, and this time it was easier to relax and just trust him. He knew someone, a longtime friend from their home church in Louisiana, who managed a working organic farm just a few minutes from where Samuel had been born and had spend the first seven years of his life. Inglewood Farm sat on roughly 3000 acres near the Red River just south of Alexandria. Originally an antebellum plantation dating back to the early 1800's, it had escaped being burned to the ground by Union troops during the Civil War because the family who resided there at the time showed kindness to a Union commander, who then gave orders for Inglewood to be protected when most of Alexandria and its surrounding plantations were destroyed. Now it was home to over 1000 acres of organic farmland, and required many field hands to work it.

It sounded ideal, but it was summertime now, and Samuel remembered how hot and humid the Louisiana summers could be. He'd think about it, maybe drive over the following weekend and just check it out. It would be a good chance to see his life-long friend Spencer, whom he hadn't seen in several years. On Friday morning that week he called Spencer to see if he'd be around and would have time to hang out. By 5:00 that afternoon, he and Khava were on their way.

Spencer and Samuel were six weeks apart and had been friends - the best of friends - as long as they both could remember. Even after his family's move to Florida when both of the boys were in first grade, they stayed in touch and had sleepovers whenever Samuel's family would return to Louisiana for holidays and during summers. They never seemed to outgrow one another and, like good friends usually do, they picked right up where they left off even after months of being apart. He knew Spencer loved him and would always, always have his back. Coming back home felt good - it was all still so familiar. On Saturday morning Spencer came in and roused

Samuel from a dead sleep and said, "Hey Sam. Let's head out to Mr. Lee's farm and have a look. I've got a good feeling about that place, for you. Come on."

Inglewood Farm was the epitome of Louisiana beauty - massive live oak trees, hanging moss, rich thick forest land carved out where vegetation grew effortlessly in the rich soil. That Saturday morning was like most every summer morning - the humidity hung perfectly still in the air above the fields, looking like clouds had dropped from their usual places above and had stopped just inches short of the ground. Being so young when they had moved to Florida, Samuel hadn't remembered enough about the uniqueness of this part of the Deep South. Today he had a newfound admiration for it. The farm offices were located inside of a century-old building with creaking wood floors and a screen door that slammed behind them when they entered. "He's to the right, there," drawled a middle-aged woman who seemed to know who they were looking for. The boys stepped toward the open door and knocked on the wooden door frame. A black head of hair laced with gray looked up to greet them. Mr. Lee was a kind man, a father of five himself, like Samuel's dad. He smiled as he recalled having Samuel's older brother Ray in his junior high Sunday School class - and said he'd be glad to give Samuel a job with pay. He was also welcome to stay in the bunkhouse, free of charge. "No dogs inside the house though," Mr. Lee said almost apologetically. "But you can sleep in the room with the window that looks out on the covered porch, where she'll most likely want to be.

That way you can see her and she can see you." He seemed to understand how strong the bond was between boy and dog. He winked and ruffled Samuel's long locks with his hand. "Glad to have ya. Tell Ray and your folks hello for me and I'll see you when you get back from Texas."

Less than a week later, the two of them - boy and dog - said their goodbyes to the Ft. Worth grandparents and headed east toward Louisiana and Inglewood Farm. Khava watched through the back window of the truck as they turned the corner and she could no longer see them. She had sensed a reluctance in their farewells, especially in their goodbyes to Samuel, and wondered if older humans had an intuitiveness that younger ones didn't. Dogs, she knew, have a keen sense of things not being quite right - a foreboding, almost a premonition. Did she just imagine it? Was she too young of a dog, like Samuel was too young of a human, to notice?

Workdays started early for the crews at Inglewood. They had to, because once the sun came up over the fields it could be blistering hot. Most of the workers either didn't own trucks or were dropped off at the farm by others each morning before dawn. Working by hand in the fields meant miles of walking during the day, only to then have to walk back to the front of the property in the afternoon sun when it was all over for the day. Samuel quickly became popular because he drove his truck out into the fields, thus providing an easy way back for the workers - as well as a shady spot for Khava while she waited for him close by. José, one of the foremen who only spoke Spanish, seemed to take a liking to Samuel - and especially to Khava. He was kind to her, slipping parts of his sandwich to her under the truck when Samuel wasn't watching. "Don't spoil her, Mr. José," he'd jokingly chide his supervisor. "She won't eat her dog food anymore if she knows she's getting people food." José's wife, Regina, was an animal lover herself and ran a rescue operation for kittens who'd been abandoned and needed to be placed. She'd find homes for her rescues, sometimes several states away, and use her own money to transport them to their new adoptive homes. Her online network had grown and José helped her when he could. Khava loved seeing her come to visit the farm, usually bringing José's lunch along with her. She knew what that meant for her.

As the long days grew almost intolerably hot on the farm, Samuel looked forward to the weekends when field work came to a halt and he could make the half hour drive with Khava to his dad's parents' home in Grant Parish, just a few miles from where his family had lived before moving to Florida. Grandma always had something on the back of the stove for him. She didn't make too much of a fuss over him being vegetarian, and she knew he loved her cornbread, rice and purple hull peas no matter how hot it happened to be outside. He could take a long shower, drink afternoon coffee on the back porch - as long as there was a hint of a breeze - play a few rounds of dominoes with Papa and go to the back bedroom with Khava and sleep like a baby. On Sundays, Grandma would pack up the leftovers and send him back to the farm with enough food for almost the whole week. He loved the weekends, and felt grateful to be able to catch up on all the lost time with them.

His family's move to central Florida had left him too young to value the uniqueness of living on almost a hundred acres, in the middle of forest land, and just a few miles from extended family. His dad's parents had lived on the same 15 acres in rural Grant Parish for several decades, almost as long as his father had been alive - in a place that had hosted far too many Thanksgiving dinners, Christmas celebrations, and Easter egg hunts to count. Grandma's house was where the coffee pot stayed on and the cookie jar was always full of butter rings you could stack up on your fingers, where rockers swayed in tandem on the back patio and stories were told over and over. Those 12 years away in Florida seemed like an eternity to Samuel, taking him from bicycles and BB guns to a wistful appreciation for what he'd left behind in the Deep South, in the dense woods of Louisiana where his roots ran several generations deep. Now at 19, he could hear the silence of the forest speaking to him and quieting his mind. He could smell the pine straw and the magnolia blooms, taste the blueberries off of Papa's bushes down at the bottom of the hill, and feel the breeze that kept the humidity from sticking to the back of his neck.

When the air stood unbearably still he could step inside to the cool air-conditioning through the kitchen door where he'd likely find his grandma standing over the stove. "Hey baby," she'd say as she slid a plate across the counter to him. It might be a slice of her signature pound cake, or a bowl of bean supreme - his dad's favorite. Whatever it was, it smelled like heaven and reminded him of how good it was to be back home.

"Home" for both of these grandparents had always been within a 20 minute drive of where they were now. Papa had been raised in nearby Summerfield, just north of Colfax, the county seat of Grant Parish. One of six children and born during the Great Depression of the 1930's - like all of Samuel's grandparents had been - Papa's daddy had been blind since the age of two when scarlet fever found its way into their Mississippi home. Moving to central Louisiana after leaving the Mississippi School for the Blind as an older teen, he'd started his own business selling brooms door-to-door, and later running a farm that would support his wife and family. He had died when Papa was only 14, but his strong work ethic was contagious and his four boys and two daughters caught it. Papa would go on to teach mathematics, coach basketball, serve as a high

Porches, Peas and Cornbread

school principal and finally retire as superintendent of the local school board.

Grandma was one of eight children born in Colfax. Her mother, lovingly referred to as "Big Mama", had been raised in south Louisiana by parents who only spoke Cajun French. She had met Grandma's father when he came down from Colfax to help build a bridge over the Atchafalaya River, and he'd married her and taken her back home with him to Colfax. The two families created an interesting blend of two cultures that would produce timeless stories for generations to come. Samuel loved hearing them. His grandparents had given him such a rich heritage, and he was just now beginning to treasure it.

But now they were getting older, and he knew one day soon he'd be telling them goodbye for a long time. Papa always talking about his faith made him feel a lot better about those goodbyes he knew he'd have to say, knowing they'd be temporary. He hoped he'd never forget what his Papa told him, and how his Grandma loved him in her unspoken ways, though he heard it loud and clear.

Spending the long days under the hot sun out at Inglewood Farm just intensified the longing Samuel had to be in the woods again. It's where he had found

Khava almost a year before, and it was where he'd spent many hours as a young boy behind his grandparents' home and at his own home back on Big Creek in Fishville. A hundred acres felt like the entire world to him then. Only 12 years later, he'd been in the woods of numerous states across the country as well as in three countries overseas. He'd seen more in his 19 years than most people see in a lifetime. And the more he saw, the more he longed to see. The forest though - the forest, where trees towered above him and created a canopy of solitude and peace for his restless, wandering heart - the forest kept calling him to come. As often as he could, he and Khava would slip off and find a trail to hike, woods to comb through, even a spot to pitch a tent for the night. Still, those Louisiana mosquitos... they were a force to be reckoned with. He'd have to find some woods with cooler, dryer temps, and he'd have to travel north to find them. His dad had talked for years about a hike together on the Appalachian Trail, and he dreamed about one day being able to just do it. Maybe he'd even invite his dad to join him for parts of it. Or his sister Rachel, who wasn't that far away in Nashville - she'd probably love doing a hike with him.

So when the day came that Mr. Lee asked

Samuel for a six month commitment to serve as a farm intern, he said he had some thinking to do about it. Six months? He hadn't stayed in the same place for six months in as long as he could remember. And on top of that, two girl interns had moved into the bunkhouse with him and, though he liked them for the most part, he didn't care much for sharing and adapting to two women who had their opinions on how a bunkhouse should be kept tidy. Tidiness was not on Samuel's priority list. Mr. Lee agreed to give him two weeks off to consider the commitment before coming back to work. He gave the boy his blessing, knowing he'd probably not see him back at Inglewood Farm again. He would be right.

Chapter 8

Where the Trail Leads

Now back at his grandparents in Grant Parish, Samuel perused the internet for places where he could find work - outside, preferably in the woods - to learn what he'd need to know for a long hike through the Appalachian mountains. He found a place in western North Carolina that sounded ideal, and made a call to the contact person - Tod, with one "d". He'd be welcome to come, but Tod would be gone until mid-August and he needed Samuel to wait until then to arrive. It was July 24th. He wasn't sure he could wait it out for the better part of three weeks. Rachel invited him to come stay with her in Nashville in the interim, but for three weeks? What would he do inside a house - again, run by women - for that long? "Okay," he told his oldest sister, "but I'll find a place in the woods to camp before then. Three weeks is way too long." He decided on a secluded campground in the northwest corner of Mississippi in the Holly Springs National Forest. That far north, the mosquitos wouldn't be as vicious and he had read about how beautiful the woods were in that area. Numerous hiking trails around a small lake looked especially appealing, so he let Rachel know what his plans were and told her that, more than likely, he'd just stay a few days and then be in Nashville by the end of the weekend. He knew he'd probably stay in the woods longer, but there was no sense in telling her that and making her worry. He had enough women who regularly worried about him, and he'd see her soon enough.

The following morning he announced to his papa what his plans were and, not even waiting for his grandma to get back from the grocery store, he loaded his things in the truck, snapped his fingers at Khava and they were off. They headed east for a couple of miles toward State Highway 165 that would take them through Monroe and finally to I-20. He gave Rachel a quick call to let her know he'd left and that he'd see her in a few days, briefly mentioning that he'd be camping at a small lake called Chewalla in northern Mississippi. He turned onto 165 headed north out of Pollock.

As he approached the second bridge out of the little town, he noticed a tall lanky figure on the side of the road, walking - but also thumbing for a lift. He'd offered rides many times to hitchhikers on his travels, dismissing the concerns his brother Ray had expressed when Samuel told him about them. "You just can't trust 'em, Dewey," he had warned. "Think about Mom and Dad, your sisters, your grandparents, all the people who love you. If you won't think about yourself, at least think about them." But Samuel had an answer, an argument for every point given, just as he always did. "Who's thinking about those folks who have to beg people passing by for a ride? If they were fortunate enough to be like me, with transportation, they'd be using it. But they aren't. Don't they deserve a chance?" He remembered again how many chances he'd been given, even when he didn't deserve them. He thought again about the kitten he'd left behind in Cameron. And anyway, he'd never had a bad experience - not once - so why would he expect anything different this time? He slowed his truck and reached over to manually roll down the window on his passenger's side.

"Where ya headed, mister?" The man, looking to

be in his early 30's, seemed surprised that Samuel had stopped and he shifted about nervously before responding. "Man, I don't really know," he finally answered. "I don't got nowhere to go, to be honest. I burned some bridges with my family and now I can't stay with them. I reckon just a ride to Monroe would be good, if you can get me there."

Samuel looked at Khava, curled up next to him in the front seat of the truck. He had a back seat but it was small, since his truck was a Chevy S-10 extended cab. No way was the guy going to fit back there. *Well,* he reasoned, *Monroe's only a couple of hours. She'll be ok between my bags back there, for that short of a time.* He snapped his fingers at her and pointed to the back. "Khava, yip!" She knew what that meant. No sooner had she hopped in the back seat than the man opened the truck door to climb in. He had nothing more than a small backpack, which he tossed over in the back seat without looking. "Welcome to my fancy ride," Samuel said to him with his signature crooked grin.

Khava didn't recognize the scent this time. Instinctively she knew this human wasn't family or part of any pack she knew, and that same sense she was having as they had pulled away from Dadad's house several weeks ago was returning. Sure, she didn't like being displaced from her usual seat in the truck - but it wasn't that. She just didn't like this man. He was nervous, and it made her nervous. Samuel didn't seem to notice a thing and chatted happily about growing up in Pollock, wondering if the man knew his older brother Ray because they were about the same age, and asking about why his family would ever think that bridges were burned in a relationship with a son and grandson. She heard Samuel talking but she kept her eyes on the man, who looked impatient and uncomfortable. If she could just sit still until the time passed and they reached Monroe.

Samuel thought a minute when the conversation lulled. He didn't know people did that. Burned bridges? He'd given his own family plenty of reasons to cut him off, to say they were done with him, but he knew they never would. He had said some harsh words to his middle sister Esther. That was months ago, and although he regretted it immediately he had said nothing. But he was sure she knew that he loved her and meant nothing by his angry ranting. The two of them had been more like each other than any of his other siblings when they were younger and honestly, they probably were now too. Esther could be as stubborn as they come, and he could too. Maybe that's why they got crossed up sometimes. But they also had the same strange sense of humor and could laugh about the most bizarre things. She was fiercely independent and afraid of nothing. He was the same. So worrying about some kind of bridge burning between the two of them was just ridiculous. The same was true with his parents. He hated thinking about all of the conflict they'd gone through with him. But there was always another chance. They believed in him, always knowing he'd come around if they just hung in there. So what was going on here? What on earth could this guy have done to deserve that? Did the family he was leaving behind know he had no place to go, nowhere to live, and obviously no way to get there? How could they just not care?

* * *

Somehow Khava had drifted off to sleep between the bags and unwelcome backpack for what must've been hours, because they were well past Monroe from the way the sun was setting as she glanced out the back window. They were heading east and the terrain was different. Her legs were stiff and she was thirsty. Samuel was no longer talking - just the usual, familiar singing under his breath - and the man's head rested against the window. He must've been sleeping. Finally the truck stopped at a roadside convenience store and she thought that surely this would be where the man would leave - but he didn't. Samuel put gas in the truck, let her out into the grass and brought her some water. Then he called her back into the truck and the three of them took off again. It would be late, much later that night before they would pull into the dark campground where she could get out and stretch her legs and hopefully be given something to eat. Samuel pitched an opened granola bar onto the ground in front of her while he was unloading sleeping bags from the truck. He seemed distant and distracted ...usually he spoke often to her, as if she understood his every word. But he hadn't said a thing directly to her since the man had joined them. Maybe the boy was just tired after a long day of driving. She wasn't sure, but she wasn't liking what she was sensing. She purposely avoided eye contact with the man. "Too late to pitch the tent," she heard Samuel say to the man. "You take the picnic table, I'll take the ground next to my dog." She was thankful to have him near, to be close to him and feel his arm reach around her and pull her close. She stretched her legs out in front of her and heard his gentle breathing in her ears, and drifted off to sleep.

The ring of Samuel's cellphone awakened her as the sun was peeking through the trees around the lake. Now she could see her surroundings - they were right on the shore of a small lake, in a picnic area, encircled by trees and already in the morning light she could see one or two fishermen launching their boats out into the water. "That was Rach," she heard Samuel say to her, but he had missed the call. He dialed her back. Turning to look over her shoulder, she noticed the man sitting atop a nearby picnic table smoking a cigarette, but well within earshot of Samuel. She could tell when Rachel answered and he began talking that he was choosing his words carefully. "No, I appreciate the offer," he told her. "But I'm at a campground that's really nice, with tons of hiking trails, so I've got all I need to stay a few days. I'll be fine. About to take Khava on a walk around this lake. See you in a bit." He made no mention to Rachel of the fact that someone was with him, and as far as Khava could tell, would be coming with them to Nashville in a few days. She hadn't been around Rachel much but she was pretty sure that wouldn't go over well. Samuel would have to figure that one out. The man lit another cigarette and she noticed on the ground in front of him there were several butts, some still faintly burning. So when Samuel hung up the phone and untied her rope from the tree, she was thankful to be going off in the woods with him. Maybe the man would find someone else he could travel with, and he'd leave them alone. But as soon as she had the thought, he hopped off the picnic table and came over to join them on their walk. Just a couple of minutes later the three of them crossed a footbridge that led over a small finger of the lake, where a lone fisherman sat still in his boat watching his motionless line. "Catchin' anything?" Samuel called down to him from the bridge. "Nothing yet," the man answered with a shrug. The boy waved and then continued on the path, leading into the woods beyond.

It was a longer walk than she'd expected but the trail hugged the shore, winding around towards the small dam at the end of the lake. Khava could see it in the distance, across the water. Samuel commented every few minutes about edible berries, stopping here and there to show the man which ones were safe to eat and which were not. The man appeared disinterested and intent on getting to wherever they were going. Khava knew already from experience that a walk in the woods with Samuel didn't necessarily have a destination or a projected arrival time - it was never about where or when they would finish. It was the journey, embracing the beauty, not being in a hurry. No agenda. Just being in the present. He stopped often, and Khava took her cue to enjoy whatever he happened to be enjoying. But as they rounded a bend that looped around a small cove in the lake, just before the dam, an overpowering scent exploded in her nostrils and she lurched to the side of the trail to look behind her and see what it was. Suddenly Samuel's hand dropped her leash, and she watched him fall facedown to the ground beside her.

Chapter 9

Beyond the Woods

As the footpath curved and climbed the ridge above a small cove in the lake, he noticed how the sound of his steps seem to fade and that a subtle breeze had begun to rustle the leaves in the canopy of trees above him. Glancing up, he was startled at the intensity of the colors and how they contrasted with the blue brilliancy of the early morning July sky. He had never noticed such beauty, even in the woods where he loved to be and felt the most at peace. Something was different, almost as if he'd stepped into an alternate reality and was seeing things for the very first time. A strange energy began to surge through him as he walked. He had the oddest sensation that he was being beckoned toward something so beautiful, so irresistible, almost magical, and his pace quickened with anticipation. What was this? The momentary distraction of movement a few yards away caught his attention. Khava had apparently picked up a scent just off the trail and was jerking at the leash. Why was she acting so erratically? He started to turn to look, but couldn't take his eyes off of what was in front of him. Standing still atop the ridge, he could see down the hill toward a steep embankment that dropped off into the cove. The early morning sunlight danced on the water down below. His senses were heightened as he stood there, taking in the beauty of his surroundings. He drew a deep breath and held it in, relishing the silence, until the heavy sound of footprints was suddenly upon him. Khava yanked the leash again and before he could turn around to look, the trees, the leaves, the sky and the water vanished into blackness.

Whose voices were those? They swirled in his head, some recognizable from somewhere in his memory, and some not. But there seemed to be many of them. Confused though he was, the voices were calm and reassuring, and he was drawn to them. He tried to see through the blackness to find faces with the voices, but couldn't. He felt the breath he'd taken in come rushing out of him in a long exhale, and his muscles relaxed into the soothing balm of the voices as warmth crept over him and the fear of uncertainty left him. There was movement, pulling and friction against the ground beneath him and then falling, falling, and then coolness and a sense of sudden weightlessness. The voices were clearer now, and whatever was happening to him in the physical realm no longer seemed significant. The irresistible beckoning from beyond was overpowering now and he gave into it, wanting to go wherever it was leading him. He didn't fight it.

The polyphony of voices dimmed, but another one rose above them - a familiar voice, though he couldn't be sure he had ever actually heard it with human ears. No, there was a hearing he had experienced that wasn't physical at all, but his soul had unmistakably heard it at different times in his life. Sometimes he had listened and even let his soul speak back to it, but other times he had ignored it. This time though, there was nothing in him that wanted to ignore it. It was all he wanted, and he listened. It whispered to him - to come. He yearned to see the source of the voice, knowing intuitively it would be the most beautiful sight he could possibly imagine, but the blackness still engulfed him. He felt his lungs sucking for air, but instead, tepid water rushed in and he knew he was sinking - down, being held down, but he had no energy left to fight it. The voice was there, whispering, and he instinctively knew the voice would not leave him. He relaxed, and trusted the voice. He knew he could.

Suddenly his eyes flew open without resistance. The glistening ripples were there again, but this time he was on the underside of them, looking up into the brightest sunlight he had ever seen. Sunlight? It wasn't the same sunlight he had watched dancing on the surface of the water just moments before. No, this light was a radiant white. He felt himself being lifted, slowly, but not by his own effort - something else lifted him up, up towards the water's surface, and then above it. Faintly, the words he'd sung a thousand times since childhood played in his head... *I was sinking....far from the peaceful shore...but the master of the waves... heard my despairing cry....from the waters lifted me, now safe am I...* Yes! He knew! For a split second he took his eyes off the light above him and glanced down, where he saw a still, lifeless figure floating in the water below him, and he knew - in that instant - that everything, everything he had ever wanted to believe, was true. The light above him grew warmer and more intense, but before he turned back and let it lift him higher, he glanced down toward the ridge where he had been standing on the path just moments before. It was now dwarfed by the vastness of what was above him. The colors of the earth, the trees, the leaves, even the blue sky were fading quickly. *But wait! Where is she? Khava! KHAVA!!* He knew he would have to leave her behind this time, though he had promised her he never would. But the voice - that reassuring voice - he knew in that moment he could trust it, even with her.

Faces flashed through his mind in milliseconds....

His parents, whom he hadn't seen since April when they took the time to drive down to Cameron to see his aquaponics system... the long hugs, the laughter, the groceries they bought him, tires they'd put on his truck, the way his mom lingered, not wanting to say goodbye.

Then his dad, whose advice he had brushed off in their last phone conversation just a week before now. "I like to learn by making my own mistakes," he remembered telling his father who was always trying to spare his son from the errors of his own ways. But all he had wanted to do was protect Samuel from the consequences of unwise choices, like most fathers genuinely want to do. Dad had tried it again, just a week or two before today, and Samuel had been overly impatient with him. Why did he have to end that phone call so abruptly? He longed for just a moment more with his dad.

His sister Rachel, who'd be waiting for him in Nashville... what would she do when he didn't show up? *Why didn't I tell her how I picked someone up on the road, and let her talk me into leaving right then?*

Then Esther, the sibling so much like himself, the one who never met a stranger and never feared a thing - he had let too much time go by without talking to her. She was off on her own adventure and he hadn't been part of it. *How would she ever know how much I've always adored her?*

And Sarah, sweet gentle Sarah... sure, they had butted heads being so close in age, but for all the years she'd put up with him, covering for him to keep him from getting in trouble, inviting him down for weekends while she was in college, and making him feel so special... he thought surely he'd have more time with her. He knew now he would not.

Then he saw his brother Ray, who'd given him chance after chance and had never, not once, given up on him... they'd had the best talk on the phone the Saturday before and laughed about things no one would understand but the two of them. And Ray had seen how much he loved Khava... and let him keep her there. He couldn't imagine having a better brother.

A rolling scroll of memories continued in front of him, almost as if he could reach out and touch them.

Four grandparents, all who loved him and made his life so rich and full.

Cousins, aunts and uncles who had poured into him and made him proud to be family with them.

His friends - Spencer, who had stuck with him through the years... John, Summer and Bailey, his closest friends in Florida who never seemed to tire of listening to him...who loved him just the way he was.

Ms. Debbie and Ms. Karen, who had loved him and cared about him like he belonged to them.

Even a few of his teachers - those who had seen past the foolishness enough to notice his qualities and gifts as an awkward and insecure kid who didn't feel like he fit in... because honestly, he didn't. Yet they saw something good in him, and appreciated his uniqueness.

They had all loved him in their broken, imperfect ways - the same broken, imperfect ways he had loved each of them. Compassion and an understanding like he'd never had before washed over him and consumed him.

Suddenly he had so much he wanted to tell each

one of them, things that had never seemed important before, but that now truly mattered. So much that had gone unspoken, unresolved, ignored... he wanted to hit the pause button and go back, to say to each face that flashed before him what he really felt. He knew how loved he had been his entire life - even when he had rebuffed that love and mistaken it for efforts to control him or make him into someone he didn't want to be. If he could just stop... and tell them... how overwhelmed he was by it all in that moment, how grateful he was for such love, and how much he loved them. All of them.

But the light - the light was too hard to resist. And the voice - he knew the same voice that was ushering him upward, away from the life below in the shadows, would speak to those he could no longer speak to if they would wait... and listen. Oh, how he wanted them all to listen! How he wished he had listened - to them, and to the voice that he recognized now as the One who had loved him completely and undeniably and unconditionally. The One who waited, patiently, as he demanded answers and explanations that never seemed to satisfy him. Of course they never satisfied him — he knew it meant he would have to surrender, and he had hated surrendering to authority. Any authority. He wanted to be free... untethered, unbound by societal norms, out from under anyone's control. Why, though? Why did he think freedom could only be experienced outside of surrender, when everything inside of him now wanted to surrender completely to this consuming love that was leading him toward the freedom he'd been straining for his entire life?

Chapter 10

Mile Marker 183

From the embankment up above Khava waited. Confused, not understanding and not grasping what had just happened below in the water, she still expected Samuel to climb up and assure her that everything was okay. Then they could leave the man behind, run back through the woods to the truck and get away. He was not a good man, and the scent still permeated the air around her that told her instincts to flee. Or to fight... why hadn't she fought? For all Samuel had done for her... why couldn't she defend him? Had she failed him?

Maybe he'd found his way back to the truck already. She had to get back before the truck left. He might be looking for her, driving around like he'd done in the Arkansas campground when he wondered where her owner had been. Yes. He would do that. But if she could just get back to the truck before he did, she could save him the search. She could at least do that much, after what she was just unable to do for him at the top of the embankment. With a surge of adrenalin she rushed back to the trail and ran as fast as she'd ever remembered running. The trail twisted and turned for what seemed like a lifetime, not the half hour it had taken the three of them to get to the place they'd stopped. Stopped? Things were quickly becoming a blur and she couldn't remember why they'd stopped walking. Oh yes. Now it came back to her. Her legs began to ache, to cramp, as she pushed her way on toward the picnic area where the truck was parked. Her eyes strained to see through the thick brush - was it still there? *Please.... Please still be there.* She knew if she could get to the truck, the boy would show up. He always came back. He promised her he'd always come back for her, and he always did. She believed him.

She gasped with relief when the truck came into view and no one was there. Samuel would surely be back, and all she had to do was wait, like she'd waited all those long days while he worked and she couldn't be right by his side. When he wasn't within sight, she could always hear his whistling from a distance, or his soothing voice singing one of those songs he had learned and sung as a child. When she reached the truck, she listened for it - but heard nothing. The woods were silent. Exhausted, she stretched out in the grass and made sure she'd be in plain sight when Samuel returned. The morning sun, now up and over the lake, glistened on the water's surface and she was grateful, even though she was panting heavily, for the warmth of it on her body. But she couldn't close her eyes and rest - she had to watch for him. She had to let him know she was there, waiting for him. Her ears were perked, waiting for the sound of his familiar whistling as he approached. It wasn't long before a figure came into her view from the direction of the trail and she fixed her attention on it. But it didn't look like the boy. There was no whistling, no singing. She waited. No, it was the same lanky, tall frame that belonged to.... Was it? The man? But he wasn't walking. He was running. Slowly, laboriously, but running. Why so slowly? As he got closer she could hear him breathing heavily. And then she could see.... He was wet, soaking wet. And covered in mud and reeds from the lake. It was then that she remembered what she'd seen happen, from the top of the embankment, in the water below. She shuddered, not wanting to believe it.

Before she could think to jump up and run, he was upon her and grabbed the leash still attached to her collar. Throwing open the door to the truck, he reached under the seat to find the key. He grabbed her around her middle and flung her up in the cab and climbed in, shutting the door and starting the engine. She frantically looked around in all directions but there was no sign of the boy. Now the scent she hated was almost unbearable but she couldn't escape it. It was right next to her in the seat, right there beside her. Fear overtook her and she closed her eyes, hoping against all hope that this nightmare would end soon and she'd open them to see her beloved friend instead, humming a tune that would calm her and assure her that everything was okay. But there was nothing.

Wildly and erratically the truck raced out of the campground and up to the main road. Twice she was thrown into the front floorboard, not able to keep her balance in the seat. Water dripping from the man's clothes sloshed everywhere and over onto her, which made it even more difficult to get traction and keep her stance. Less than two minutes up the road, she noticed a crew of men in orange vests with shovels, and felt the truck slow down as it approached. The man rolled down his window quickly and an older gentleman with a kind, soft face peered inside, looking puzzled. "How do I get back to the main highway?" The now suspicious older man pointed in front of him and then gestured to turn right at the stop sign. "Son, is everything okay?" He asked from outside, obviously noticing the man he was speaking to was soaking wet and extremely agitated. But a response didn't come, and the window rolled up. He was in a hurry, and the man on the road crew didn't know why. But Khava did.

Apparently he'd made a wrong turn, but a small store was up ahead where he could surely get directions - so he turned the truck into the parking lot, jumped out and shut the door behind him. There was no way for her to get out. Within minutes they were up on the main highway and she hadn't a clue where they were going. All she knew was the boy wasn't with her and she would have to find a way to get back to the campground to be with him, to help him, to rescue him. She knew he needed her, and more than that, she knew she needed him.

She must have drifted off to sleep for awhile, still exhausted from the mad dash back to the truck and from the terror of what she feared was really true, of what had happened an hour before. When the truck came to a slow crawl on the shoulder of the interstate, she was barely aware of what was happening when the man's arm reached across her and unhooked her collar from her neck, tossing it to the floor with the leash still attached to it. Opening the door she was pressed up against, he then pulled his leg up into the seat beside her and pushed her hard with his foot, sending her out the door and onto the pavement below. Before she could gather her wits to stand up, he sped off and away from her. The truck door slammed shut as she watched it pull back into the lane and soon go out of sight. She glanced around her, watching vehicles fly past, some missing her by inches. Dazed and frightened, she turned in the direction they'd come from and began walking. A car coming over the crest of the hill in front of her didn't see her in time, and before she had time to lunge out of its way, everything went black.

For a time, she was back home, on the farm, lying in the tall grass next to her mother. Crickets chirped nearby, and the sun warmed her coat. She could hear the sound of her own breathing, not wanting to open her eyes and spoil the moment. But another sound, loud and intrusive, roared in her ears - what was that? Squinting to see in the glare of sunlight, she saw the sound and remembered where she had been when the lights went out. Somehow the force of impact had thrown her at least a dozen feet off the shoulder of the road, into the tall grass, mercifully placing her out of more harm's way and providing at least partial camouflage from passersby. It must have been mid-to-late afternoon because the warmth she felt from the sun was intense. It was late July, the hottest time of the summer. She'd have to find some shade, and desperately needed to hydrate. Attempting to raise herself up, a burning sensation pierced her left front leg and she dropped back down into the grass, unable to get up. She looked down at it, twisted and bent in the wrong direction. The burning traveled down her left side and she let her eyes wander back over her body to see what was causing it. A large patch of her coat was missing and though it wasn't much, there was still enough blood to invite flies to the site. She tried to move her head enough to lick the wound but couldn't reach it. The pain from her badly broken leg was now radiating throughout her body, so she sat in the grass, still hoping - by some miracle - that she'd see the boy pull up in his truck and that he'd come rescue her. He had promised.

She waited, keeping her head up so he could see

her. Hours went by and she watched the light fade into blackness. Fewer cars passed by now, and she felt hopelessness creeping in, just like she did a year before, in the campground, after returning time and time again to the place where the farmer's truck had left her. But this time she didn't have the strength to push through it. No, too much had happened, and she knew in her heart that Samuel would not be back. He would've wanted to, would've done everything in his power to get to her, to save her - but in her soul, she knew he was gone. Night came and morning dawned, and she picked up her head one last time.

As the morning light brought her surroundings into clearer view, an SUV appeared to slow down as it passed her and she could see a woman inside - the driver - turning to look in her direction. The vehicle pulled onto the shoulder of the highway, almost stopping. Still, Khava couldn't move. What was the lady doing? Did she notice her lying there, with ears perked, watching? Now she seemed to be looking intently at something in her hand, and her fingers were moving rapidly. Khava had seen Samuel do it before, on his phone.

8:00am:

Amy: "Hey there was a dog at mile marker 183 - actually just south of mile marker 183 that I'm not sure hadn't been hit by a car. He is off the side of the road on the south bound side of 55. Is that anywhere near you? It looked like a German Shepherd"

Scott: "Yes that is right at Winona. I work in Greenwood about 30 miles away, what condition did the fellow appear to be in? I know a vet/rescue in Winona that I could get to go and help. Thanks for alerting me Amy!"

Amy: "It was like he was just lying in the grass (he was sitting up) but it dawned on me he might be hurt"

Scott: "Thanks Amy.. I alerted WAAG (Winona animal advocate group) to see if someone can go out and check on him... he/she could be dehydrated and lost too, there's no telling"

After the SUV drove away, she put her head down and wished herself into a deep sleep. Maybe, just maybe, she'd wake up in that field of flowers with her mother, her leg wouldn't hurt, and in the distance she'd see him coming for her - whistling his happy tune, keeping his promise to her. She felt her breathing slow down, and knew she would see him soon.

Her dream was interrupted by the slamming door of a large van with the letters WAAG scrawled on the side of it. Two men approached her slowly, but they were gentle and she picked up a faint scent telling her there was nothing to fear. She didn't much care at this point, but it would be nice not to die under worse circumstances than she'd already lived through.

"Let's take a look at ya, girl," one of the men spoke softly to her. "Yep, she's been hit alright. That leg is a mess for sure," he told the other one, who came toward her with a large blanket. "We'll get you wrapped up and in the van, and you'll be taken care of. Don't you worry. Poor ol' thing." The pain was excruciating when they lifted her up, put her on the blanket and carried her to the van. But she didn't whimper or growl. She knew these were good people, trying to help. Like her Samuel always was. And anyway, she didn't have the strength or will to fight them. She couldn't keep her eyes open as the van pulled away and back onto the interstate, so she drifted off to sleep and kept watch for her mother in the field again.

Probably a half hour or so later, several people unloaded her from the van and carried her inside a small building that smelled of a lot of other animals - dogs, cats, even horses. One kind man in particular stayed with her when she was taken to a room and then was laid on a cold metal table. "Hi sweet girl," he whispered to her. "My name is Dr. Hill, and I'm going to make you feel better. I don't know who you are, where you've come from or what exactly has happened to you, but it's okay. You're in safe hands now." She believed him. He was tender with her, and when he spoke he looked directly into her eyes. Only Samuel and his brother Ray had done that with her. Her eyelids were too heavy to keep open, and after feeling the sting of the needle in her shoulder, she gave in and let go.

11:13am:

Amy: "Do you know if they found him?"

Scott: "I'm not sure.. I'll give them a call and check"

Scott: "He's at the vet, they got him and are working on him as well as trying to locate his owner.. you're right he'd been hit"

Amy: "Oh geez - let me know where I can donate"

Scott: "Winona Animal Hospital. Thanks!"

Amy: "Noooo - thank yall"

Scott: "You're welcome glad to help"

Amy: "I'm eating lunch but I'll call in a donation shortly"

Scott: "That's an awesome thing to do. I know that will be greatly appreciated"

Chapter 11

Through a Window in Heaven

He had no idea how much time had passed since that day. All of those who had flashed across his memory as he was leaving were still in his conscious mind, but now he saw them all through a different lens. It wasn't that they were less important to Samuel. They just paled in comparison to everything in this new realm - this realm that he had seen glimpses of when he was paying attention in his former life, but they would vanish before he could really absorb them.

He would've liked to somehow be able to get word to some of them, even just one of them, to describe what he'd just experienced and what was happening every second of his existence on this side - but he knew there'd be no earthly words for any of it.

He remembered the times he attempted to imagine what it would be like - all the questions he had that simply went unanswered, or left him frustrated and wanting to know more - but now he understood why. He couldn't have fathomed, in a million years or with the deepest insight or the most intellectually advanced mind, what this was like. Time meant nothing where he was now, except that he realized how limiting it had been to live by measures and increments of it. Here, he had learned already, absolutely nothing has an end - so there's no need for time. *Funny*, he thought to himself, *how finally having enough of it where it never runs out makes it completely unnecessary.* He loved that everything here was in the moment - no sadness for circumstances of the past, no longing for events in the future. Every moment held in it a lifetime of joy, love, and gratitude.

He'd seen glimpses of what was happening in the realm he'd just left, but viewing them all from a new perspective made him see everything so differently than how he knew his family was experiencing them. There were the flashes in time, since his departure, that were hard to watch - the sadness, the horror, the agony - knowing he could do nothing to help them, nothing to tell them they were only seeing, as he remembered the Scriptures saying, "through the glass dimly." But they would see and understand soon enough. He also realized that he now had the keen ability to be able to see beyond their todays - he could see how they would learn to adapt, to absorb their grief and let it change them into stronger, better people. Time was critical in that other realm, the one he had just left, and time is what it would take for each of them to recover.

When he watched as his mother wept in agony over her open Bible, pleading to know that her boy had not been abandoned by God and left to suffer in the water that day, he knew she would get her answer. She was looking in the right place, and she found it.

When his dad wandered through the woods behind Papa's house the morning of the funeral, begging God to somehow give him a heart of forgiveness for whoever had taken his son's life, he knew God would give it to him.

When his sisters relentlessly spread the news through their social media posts and asked everyone everywhere to pray that Khava would, by some miracle, be found, he knew already that God was at work to bring her to his family. He smiled, knowing that his mom would research the name "Khava" in the weeks to come, and would discover the Hebrew word QAVAH - which means "waiting with expectant hope". He knew what that would mean to his mother, how it would sustain her through the years that would follow as she waited for their reunion. He knew Khava would be a gift to his broken-hearted family. They needed her... and she needed them. They would be her pack, and his promise to her would be unbroken.

In the brief time since his arrival in heaven he had already encountered his dad's friend, Pat Cannon, whose life on earth had ended barely a week after his had. She had finished her battle with cancer. Just before her death she had received the email Dad had sent to her, when he got word that she wouldn't live much longer.

Pat,

Know that you are in our prayers!

When you get to the other side, please give this message to our 19 year old son who went home to be with the Lord last week. His name is Samuel Deward Smith.
    Samuel,

I'm very proud of you. I'm sorry that I didn't tell you that enough.

I'm very proud of who you are and how God made you.

We miss you and will see you soon. Ask Jesus to let us know that you got this message.

Also, please ask him to help us find Khava so I can take care of her for you.

I love you, my son. Dad.

He wished he could shout down to his dad below, "Dad! I got it! I got the message and Khava's waiting for you! Wait Dad. Just wait. *Qavah!*"

For 14 days - but for what only seemed like a moment to him - he watched as his sisters blanketed their social media sites with posts. News articles on what had happened at Chewalla Lake, surveillance videos of a suspect still not apprehended, photos of Khava, photos of him with her - hundreds and hundreds of friends shared their posts and asked others to share them. In the small, quaint town of Holly Springs, Mississippi, compassionate citizens gathered together and combed through acres and acres of wooded area around nearby Chewalla Lake, hoping someone would spot Khava. Samuel watched as his family received an outpouring of love and grace they could never have imagined. He was thankful.

And finally, three weeks after Khava had been left on the highway, a veterinary assistant in the Winona Animal Hospital opened up her Facebook app on her cellphone. There it was in her newsfeed - the story about the murder of the boy, and the dog - the same dog who'd been lying in a kennel in the back of the office, not eating, mostly sleeping, medicated to relieve her pain - and obviously grieving, for some reason. Now the assistant knew why. When the phone rang in the Marshall County sheriff's office a few minutes later, the sheriff's deputy nearly dropped the receiver. "What a miracle," he managed to say to the woman. "I'll verify the photo with the family, but I'm sure it's her. It'll take me an hour, but I'll be down there to get her. Thank you!"

Word traveled quickly among family and friends near and far. A call was made to Dr. Hill, thanking him profusely for keeping Khava alive and out of pain. He warned Samuel's family that she would need extensive surgery, but he felt a good orthopedic veterinary surgeon could do it.

When Samuel's parents asked Dr. Hill for the details of how Khava had gotten to his clinic, he told the story about the kind woman who requested she be picked up and cared for, and how she then paid the clinic enough money to keep Khava there until her family could find her. He gave them the woman's number, and she received the call that every Good Samaritan dreams of getting. Later that day, she posted on her Facebook page:

Aug 14, 8:18pm:

"Right place, right time - I was on my way to Jackson a few weeks ago for a meeting when I saw this dog lying off on the right side of the road in the grass off I-55 outside of Winona. Turns out she had been hit by a car. I called my friend in the area - (S.R.) - and he called in the cavalry. The police showed up and she was taken to the vet and has remained there through the good graces of many folks. Fast forward to this morning when I received an unexpected call. Turns out she belonged to the man who was murdered at Chewalla Lake a couple of days before i saw her, it appears. The man's parents contacted me this morning to tell me her

story. The man's family has been searching frantically for his beloved dog, Khava, ever since he was killed. Thanks to sharing on Facebook, her family found her all the way from Louisiana to North Mississippi. They are on the way to pick up their son's dog. We spoke for quite awhile on the phone and they are very sweet people. Please pray for them. So happy these people can find some measure of peace."

From a cloud of witnesses above - Samuel, alongside his people who had gone before him, generations in front of him, who now were gathered around him - a cheer went up that reverberated across the heavens.

Chapter 12

A Promise Kept

It was late in the afternoon. She could tell by the way the sunlight streamed in the window, though she had no idea how long she'd been there or if she'd ever leave. So many times she wished she could will herself to die, but the desire to live surpassed it. A sliver, a thread of hope each day - she wondered where it came from. Maybe one day, she'd know.

The events of the last three weeks blurred together in Khava's mind. Loneliness - the same enemy she had battled while alone in that Arkansas campground - crept over her like a disease, depleting her of an appetite to eat or move around any more than what she had to do to keep her injured leg from cramping. Sleep was all she wanted to do, because sleep brought with it dreams of her mother and vivid images of the boy she had grown to love and depend upon. And he had promised - he had shown her the sunsets, and talked about God's signs of His promises in the skies - and she had believed him. She couldn't forget it, nor did she want to.

Days passed, each one being the same as the one before. There were kind, gentle people there in the building who stopped and reached into in her kennel to pet her, check her food bowl, and coax her out to the grassy area - but she never wanted to linger. The grass and fresh air just reminded her of what she missed, of what she had lost and would never have again. She watched as other dogs were removed from their kennels and didn't return. Where had they gone? Sometimes she'd hear the voices of people and excited cries from those dogs, jubilant sounds of reunions, and she couldn't bear it. Hers would not come.

One late afternoon though, the office up front was unusually loud and she listened intently for a clue to what the reason might be. The kind lady at the desk had excitement in her voice as she called for Dr. Hill, then beckoned the others to come look... come and see.... what? A scent, ever so faint, wafted into the room where her kennel sat and she knew something good, very good, was happening. The noise fell quiet for at least an hour, maybe two... and then picked up again. She could make out voices, new voices she'd not heard in the clinic before, and then finally the door to the kennel room opened. Two men in uniforms stepped in and leaned down to peer into her kennel. At first she was frightened, but the scent wasn't alerting her to fear - and then both men smiled at her. One began wiping tears from his eyes, and the other spoke softly to her. "We've got you, sweet girl. Your family has been looking for you without giving up, and now you've been found. Let's get you home to your people."

Her people? Were these Samuel's people? Would they want her.... Would they love her... would they be anything like Samuel?

The ride from Winona to the Marshall County Sheriff's Office felt surreal to her. The two uniformed men were talking excitedly on their phones and to each other, and both of them kept reaching back to touch her reassuringly. She had no idea where she was headed, but she felt safe. The pain in her leg throbbed even more as her heart raced, but she knew something was happening that centered on her. Unable to close her eyes and sleep in the backseat, she finally felt the vehicle come to a stop and heard the engine shut off. The deputy carried her into his office, laid her down on the floor beside his desk and made a phone call. "She's ready when you are, Rachel," Khava heard him say. "We'll see you and Sarah shortly." The names she didn't recognize at first. Or did she? She waited. She hoped.

Finally, the kind deputy led her outside to the parking lot, where two girls - women, but young - like Samuel - stood waiting at a distance. They waved, arms around one another, and waited as Khava and the deputy approached, slowly. Something was drawing her to these girls. Had she seen them somewhere before? Did she know them? How would she have known them? The walk across the empty lot seemed to take too long but she kept her gaze fixed on the two in front of her, who were now crying and hugging one another as they watched her approach. Somehow she forgot about the pain radiating down her leg when the unmistakably familiar scent reached her - it was his scent! Limping, her pace picked up and she ran - as best she could - to what she knew now was her pack. Samuel's sisters embraced her amidst tears of joy, sobs of grief, and then laughter. Khava could hear his voice in all of it. His smell, that family scent, covered them and she knew - in that moment - that he had kept his promise.

Everything about these two that had come for her - their tender voices, the way they stared long into her eyes, as if looking for something - or someone - told her that he hadn't forgotten her, he had remembered his promise to her, and he'd done the best he could to keep it.

The car door opened and the men carefully lifted her weak, frail body up into the back seat. Khava watched as they hugged the two sisters, wiped tears away and stepped back to see them off. Almost reverently, the three of them sat in the car for several minutes, looking at one another, perfectly still except for eyes shifting from one to the other. "Samuel," one of the girls finally spoke out loud. "Thank you." The affirmation they felt in the silence was palpable.

Within just a few minutes they had pulled up onto the highway leading back to Nashville, and the inside of the car grew quiet. But Khava listened. From the front seat, just above the steady whirring of the tires on the pavement, she heard it. Rachel was humming something softly, and Khava recognized the song.

Afterword

Khava returned with Samuel's sisters to Nashville, where they were joined a few days later by the rest of the Smith family. She received treatment for her injuries at Blue Pearl Pet Hospital in Franklin, TN, and a successful surgery was performed under the compassionate and highly skilled hand of Dr. Kevin Au. Her recovery lasted for several weeks, but her health has been completely restored. She now lives with us at our home in Waco, Texas.

On July 26, 2017 Samuel Deward Smith, at the age of 19, was attacked from behind and forcibly drowned in a shallow cove near the dam of Chewalla Lake in the Holly Springs National Forest of Marshall County, Mississippi. He had gone there to camp, to hike, and to enjoy the woods with his beloved companion Khava. His body was discovered by fishermen four days later.

Two weeks after the murder, Samuel's killer was identified on the security video at the Lake Center convenience store as he was leaving the area of Chewalla Lake. Although law enforcement had his name and information, he managed to allude them for three months, never leaving the state of Mississippi. On October 30, 2017 he walked into the sheriff's office in Humphries County and turned himself in, saying that he was tired of running.

In our family's case - and sadly we know it doesn't happen this way for everyone - the judicial system worked just as it is meant to work. It took almost four years from the day of the murder, but on July 23, 2021, a jury in Holly Springs found him guilty of capital murder and sentenced him to life without parole. He is serving his sentence in the Mississippi state prison system.

As a follower of Jesus I am called to forgive my enemy, regardless of whether or not he has asked me for it. By God's grace and with His help, I have done so - thereby setting myself free from a prison far worse than the one in which my son's killer lives.

There is mercy for all at the foot of the cross, and room enough for him, too. I pray daily for his repentance and restoration, and that one day God will use the story of my son's sacrifice as a powerful testimony through this man.

Samuel is very much alive and well in heaven. I will join him there, when the days God has ordained for me are finished. How do I know this, for certain? Because of the gospel, the good news that simply tells me this: that God loved the world so much that He gave His only Son - Jesus - so that whoever believes in Him will not perish, but will have eternal life. (John 3:16).

We are saved by grace - through faith - it is nothing, and never will be, that we can do. It is simply God's gift to us, and we can either receive it or we can reject it. It was God's gift to Samuel, and he accepted it.

I know the day will come when Khava will cross her rainbow bridge and we will have to say goodbye to her. Her purpose in this life will have been accomplished - providing loyal companionship to Samuel in the last year of his life, and bringing inexplicable comfort to us, his family. I can't be sure of it, but something in my soul tells me that a reunion will take place one sunny day in a wide open field where the grass is lush and green, and she will look - toward the crest of a hill - to see the source of the song she knows so well.

Samuel with his dad in Cameron, TX. April 2017

Samuel and Khava, June 2017

Sheriff Dickerson and Maj. Kelly McMillen with Khava August 14, 2017

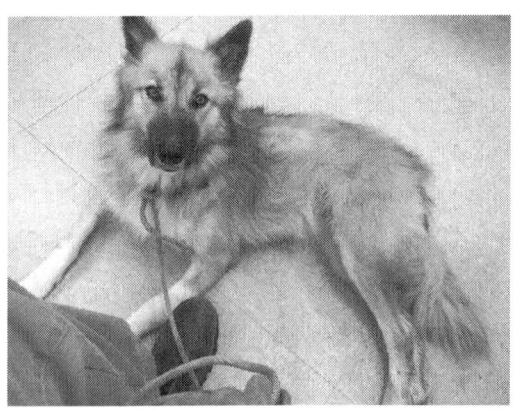

Waiting for the girls at the Marshall County sheriff's office August 14, 2017

Meeting Amelia to thank her September 6, 2017

Beth and Khava April 2018

Sarah, Rachel, Ray and Esther July 14, 2018

Dale, Beth and Ray at the close of the trial with Marshall County District Attorney Ben Creekmore, Maj. Kelly McMillen and Assistant DA Christine Tatum July 23, 2021

Photo Gallery

Thankful for a verdict that brought justice for Samuel July 23, 2021

Chewalla Lake in Holly Springs National Forest July 24, 2021

Khava today

Acknowledgments

I am deeply and eternally grateful for the community of God's people who have walked us through trauma, grief and healing. We've been blessed with family and fellow believers who have loved us well. This list could never be complete but I'd like to thank the following:

The Marshall County Sheriff's Department: specifically, Kelly McMillen and Sheriff Dickerson;

Christine Tatum and Ben Creekmore of the Marshall County District Attorney's office;

The wonderful citizens of Holly Springs, MS who searched for Khava and then loved us and cared for us during the trial;

The men and women of Marshall County who served with integrity on the jury;

Amelia Amy Lavorn, who spotted Khava on I-55 and was instrumental in saving her life;

Dr. Daniel Hill and his staff at Winona Veterinary Clinic in Winona, MS;

Dr. Don Corley, for encouraging me to write - and wisely knowing it would be my therapy;

Debby Kerr-Henry and Karen Howington, my dear friends and Samuel's "other mothers";

Kim Schwan Littlewood, my best friend of over 50 years who knows the song in my heart and sings it to me when I've forgotten the words;

The community of believers at Kingsville Baptist Church, Pollock First Baptist, Grace Oviedo and Highland Baptist Church who have loved us and supported us;

Our parents, siblings and our other four children who loved Samuel unconditionally;

My husband Dale, who is waiting with expectant hope - "QAVAH!" - alongside me every day;

And finally, my Lord Jesus Christ. Without Him our loss, our story, and our lives would be in vain. Instead, He is redeeming them and is making all things new.

Hallelujah! Come quickly, Lord Jesus.

And see you in the morning, sweet Samuel.

About the Author

Beth Baird Smith is a fourth generation native of central Texas. Born in Dallas, she moved with her family to Austin and later to Waco, where she earned a Bachelor of Science degree in Education from Baylor University in 1981. She married her college sweetheart, began teaching school and was widowed as a young mother before the age of 26. Several years following her remarriage, Beth and husband Dale sold their home in rural Louisiana and moved with their children to join the staff of Campus Crusade for Christ in Orlando, Florida where they served with two different international ministries for almost 20 years. In 2010 Beth was diagnosed with stage 3 breast cancer, choosing a holistic treatment path that proved successful and has allowed her to remain healthy. Together she and Dale have raised five children who now live in Florida and California, and they have two grandchildren. Beth now resides in Waco, Texas where she and Dale are co-founders of a non-profit ministry to unreached language groups called Jesus Said Go (www.Jesus-said-go.com). She spends much of her spare time mentoring and discipling young women in their local community and pursuing a variety of writing projects. She also speaks at women's conferences and retreats, sharing her life experiences of grief, forgiveness and healing. She can be contacted at beth@jesus-said-go.com.

Made in the USA
Columbia, SC
08 August 2023